WHAT'S THE BIG IDEA?

What's the Big Idea? focuses on the hottest issues and ideas around. In a nationwide survey, we asked young people like you to tell us which subjects you find most intriguing, worrying and exciting.
The books in this series tell you what you need to know about the top-rated topics.

Books available now:
The Mind
Virtual Reality
Women's Rights
Animal Rights
The Environment
Nuclear Power
Time and the Universe
Religion
Genetics

Books coming soon:
Food
Alien Life
The Media
The Paranormal

We would love to hear what you think. If you would like to make any comments on this book or suggestions for future titles, please write to us at:

What's the Big Idea?
Hodder Children's
338 Euston Road
London NW1 3B

D0227253

Published by Hodder Children's Books 1998

10 9 8 7 6 5 4 3 2 1

ISBN 0 340 70877 8

A Catalogue record for this book is available from the
British Library.

Printed by Mackays of Chatham plc, Chatham, Kent

Hodder Children's Books
A division of Hodder Headline plc
338 Euston Road
London NW1 3BH

Genetics

Martin Brookes
Illustrated by Nick Dewar

h
Hodder
Children's
Books

a division of Hodder Headline plc

For Mum and Dad, with love.
MB

to Srilatha Vuthoori
for running up my phone bill and
controlling the mutants. ND.

Contents

clonin in the øloqmin ♫ ♪

* **Clone** and other words in bold type are explained in **What the words mean**. Names in bold are in **Who's who**.

Variety is the spice of life

Have you ever thought of yourself as being a bit different from everyone else, unique? Well, this isn't just wishful thinking. Unless you have an identical twin, there really isn't anyone else who looks exactly the same as you do. There are more than five billion people on the earth and every one of us is a totally unique human being!

Of course, you're more similar to some people than to others. Have a look at your brothers or sisters, your parents or any other relatives that you've got. You probably have more physical features in common with them than you do with your unrelated friends.

The big question is where do all these differences and similarities between you and everyone else come from?

from your genes! —

Your **genes** are a remarkable recipe for your body. They are a set of coded instructions inside you which help to make you the way you are and look. Your genes are inherited from your parents, one half coming from your mother and one half from your father. That's why we often resemble our parents, brothers and sisters - we share similar genetic recipes.

Genetics is the basis of the similarities and differences, not just between people, but all living things.

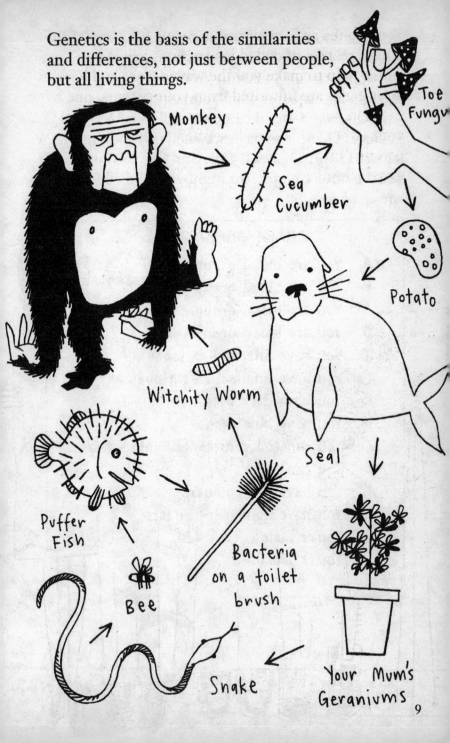

Monkey

Sea Cucumber

Toe Fungus

Potato

Witchity Worm

Seal

Puffer Fish

Bacteria on a toilet brush

Bee

Snake

Your Mum's Geraniums

9

Still not convinced about your uniqueness? Then have a look at the biological individuality chart on the opposite page. Starting from the centre, mark the adjacent squares which correspond to your own characteristics. For example, if your blood group is O and you have attached earlobes, mark square O and square T. Carry on like this for each feature until you get to a number at the edge of the chart.

CHART CHARACTERS

A   You are blood group A

B   You are blood group B

AB You are blood group AB

O   You are blood group O

(you may have to ask your parents what blood group you are)

T   You have attached earlobes

t   You have unattached earlobes

B   You have dark eyes

b   You have blue eyes

C   You can roll your tongue into a tube

c   You can't

H   You have hairy fingers

h   You have non-hairy fingers

♂   You're male

♀   You're female

dark eyes

unattached earlobes

attached earlobes

non rolling tongue →

blue eyes

hairy finger

tongue rolling

hairless finger ↑

Biological Individuality Chart

Try the chart on your friends or relatives.
It's extremely unlikely that you'll end up
with the same number as any of them.
And that's using only six characteristics
to describe yourself. Humans have about
100,000 genes! Imagine how many
different possible combinations there
would be if you used 100,000
characteristics instead of six.

ask me. I do
free blood
tastes. I mean
tests.

FLAP
FLAP

I ken nowt about Genetics

Genetics is one of the newest of all the sciences. It's really only in this century that we have begun to understand why people look similar to - or different from - one another. Modern genetics is beginning to reveal the previously hidden recipes within ourselves and within all living creatures. Knowing about our genetic recipes can tell us why we are how we are, and can even predict our futures. It's no wonder that genetic discoveries make the news - nearly every day!

today on Genetics TV we shall engineer me a wife

NEWSAGENT

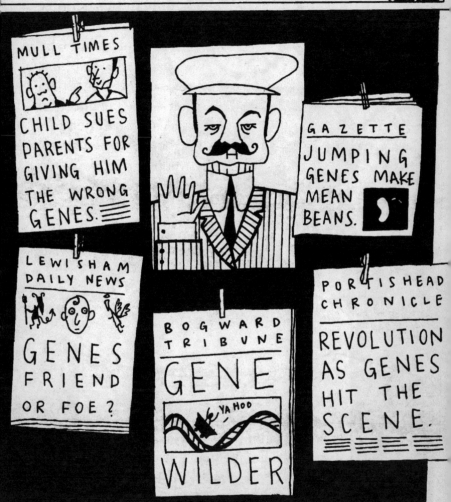

MULL TIMES
CHILD SUES PARENTS FOR GIVING HIM THE WRONG GENES.

GAZETTE
JUMPING GENES MAKE MEAN BEANS.

LEWISHAM DAILY NEWS
GENES FRIEND OR FOE?

BOGWARD TRIBUNE
GENE
YAHOO
WILDER

PORTISHEAD CHRONICLE
REVOLUTION AS GENES HIT THE SCENE.

Speak for yourself. Some of us have it and some of us don't.

Humans are not just machines at the mercy of their genes. The relationship between you and your genes is a bit like that between a cake and its recipe. To bake a good cake you need the right recipe, but you also need all the ingredients and the right cooking conditions - the right temperature. The recipe doesn't make the cake on its own. Likewise, a genetic recipe on its own doesn't make a person.

So the reason we're all different from one another isn't just because of our genes, although that's important. It's also because of the unique way each of us is brought up - our environment. Each of our lives comprises a unique set of genes and a unique set of family and social experiences. Even identical twins, which share an identical set of genes with one another, aren't exactly alike. Every one of us is a product of *nature* (your genes) and *nurture* (your environment).

WOLF CHOSE to dedicate himself to his career. Is wealthy beyond reproach. Has a loving wife and child. Wishes he was his brother.

NORMAN CHOSE a life of loose living on the road. Lost all his money gambling on Newts. Is unable to commit to a relationship. Wishes he was his brother.

CASE STUDY: TWINS AGED 35.

Some features, like our sex and the colour of our eyes and hair, are coded entirely by our genes. On the other hand, your decision to read this book or your liking for a particular band has nothing to do with genetics whatsoever! Other things like our weight, height and intelligence are shaped by a mixture of our genes and our environment. If we all ate the same amount of food, some of us would still be heavier than others because of our different genetic recipes. Even so, if you spend your life eating masses of burgers, chips and cake, you'll end up fat, no matter what your genes say!

See how many differences you can spot between the two people shown below, and then have a guess at whether you think those differences are caused by genes, the environment, or a mixture of the two.

B.

A.

SCIENCE TEACHER
"WHACKO JACKO"

SCIENCE TEACHER
"MAVIS"

Answers:

Genes	**Environment**	**Mixture**
wine colour	wine preference	weight
hairy fingers	tie shape	teeth
ear hairiness	shoes	height
		general hairiness

Before anyone knew anything about genetics, people were convinced that children resembled their parents simply because of shared environments or experiences. This led to some bizarre behaviour.

My father cleans the sewers

In ancient Greece, pregnant women were advised to look at noble statues and other beautiful objects to impart beauty to their children.

In nineteenth century France, pregnant women believed it was their duty to wander round the Louvre art gallery, admiring the fine paintings, so that their children would be born beautiful.

I like the Mountain pictures best.

In East Anglia, pregnant mothers were advised not to eat strawberries because it would cause a strawberry coloured birthmark on the baby's skin.

Many of the myths about inheritance disappeared when people became aware of genetics in the early part of this century. But the early geneticists were mainly rich and powerful men, who seemed more concerned about using genetics to support their existing prejudices than actually understanding the scientific details. The study of human genetics was founded by **Francis Galton**, the cousin of Charles Darwin. Galton was convinced that genetics could explain all human differences. This was convenient for those in power because now the problems of society could be blamed on genes rather than society itself.

fig one.
↓

an outy belly button.

Galton believed that people were criminals, poor or needy because they were biologically inferior. He founded the **eugenics** movement - set up to improve the biological quality of the human race. In practice, this meant discouraging or preventing anyone who was poor, a criminal or of low intelligence from having any children, and encouraging the rich and powerful to have more children.

Galton's name (although not his ideas!) lives on today in the form of the Galton Laboratory of genetics at University College London.

Today, it's easy to dismiss Galton's ideas, but at the time, Galton's views were popular with those who shared his wealth and influence. And the consequences were appalling.

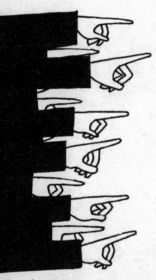

In the United States, eugenics was used to persecute anyone who didn't fit in to the norms of society. Homosexuals, criminals, the mentally ill, people of low intelligence and communists were all classified as genetically inferior. Thousands of people were sterilized to prevent them having children and passing on their genes.

UNCLE SAM STANDS TRIAL

Later, eugenics had even worse applications in Germany. As well as executing people with mental and physical disabilities, Hitler attempted to exterminate all Jews, partly because he believed that they were genetically inferior. Over six million people were killed because of one man wielding his power and prejudice over an entire nation.

So the early days of genetic science have a bad record. And today, for many people, the mention of genetics still conjures up images of Nazi Germany. But modern genetics is concerned with understanding the scientific truth behind life's variety and complexity, rather than using science for political ends. Now, genetics has more to do with improving the quality of life rather than destroying it: genetics is of use in medicine and agriculture. But although it can offer many benefits to our lives, genetics is still a controversial science.

In search of the genes

To find out where our genes are and how they work, we've got to delve under the skin.

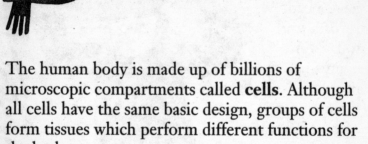

The human body is made up of billions of microscopic compartments called **cells**. Although all cells have the same basic design, groups of cells form tissues which perform different functions for the body.

Skin cells give your body protection, muscle cells enable you to move, bone cells give you support, and blood cells transport oxygen around the body.

I do thoughts

I do toe nails

And these different tissues can be grouped together to form organs such as the heart and lungs, all of them essential for the human body to function properly.

Since we all start life as a single cell which divides over and over again to produce the final count of billions, how is it that different cells do different jobs? It comes back to genes - of course.

Genes can be turned on and off like light switches. Although every cell within one person has the same set of genes, not all genes work at the same time. The combination of genes which are switched on in one cell make it work differently from another cell with a different combination switched on.

Hello, we are shallow props to guide you through the baffling maze of Genetics

PROFESSOR JEAN SHRINKMEISTER ←

COLIN LEARNALOT ←

Inside the cell, there is an inner compartment called the **nucleus**, which contains long, thin, thread-like structures called **chromosomes**. Our genes are arranged on the chromosomes like beads in a necklace.

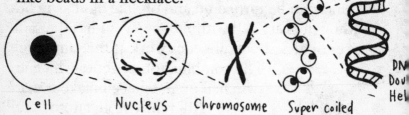

Cell   Nucleus   Chromosome   Super coiled DNA   DNA Double Helix

Chromosomes come in pairs. Humans have 23 pairs of chromosomes, making 46 in total. One chromosome in each pair comes from your mother, one from your father. One particular pair, the sex chromosomes, is especially interesting. Sex chromosomes come in two types called X and Y. If you're female you have two Xs.

But males have one X paired with one Y. So it's this Y chromosome which determines that someone is a boy, and it always comes from the father, since the mother doesn't have one to pass on.

X   Y

I like the look of your Y's.

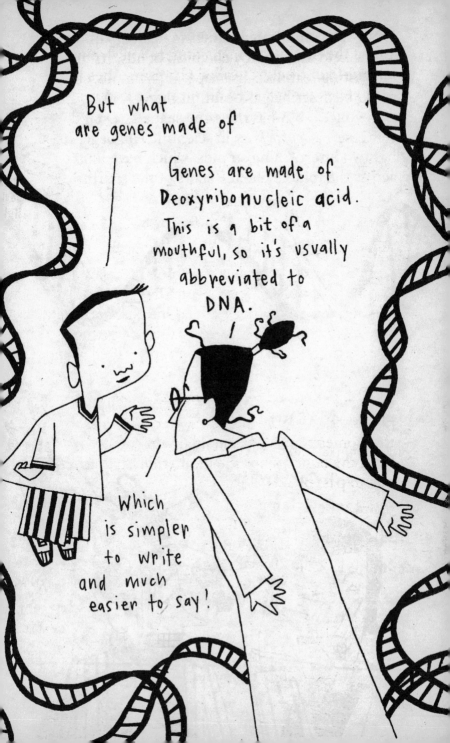

DNA is a complicated molecule made up of lots of atoms held together by chemical bonds. Its most interesting feature is its shape. If any molecule could be described as beautiful then DNA is the one! DNA has the same shape as a spiral staircase - a *double helix* in scientific language. It has two intertwining strands, which have links across the middle like the stairs of the staircase.

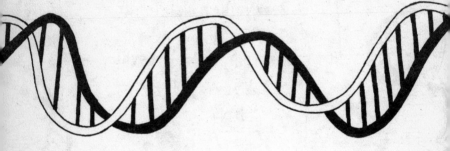

TRULY MAGNIFICENT!
Such daring use of roundy
bits with a tweak
of condescension
balancing the
modernist ethic.

MR. PANTS
top art
critic

DNA is a molecular code or language, found in virtually all living things, from bacteria to humans. But unlike the English language, which has 26 letters, A to Z, the language of DNA is made up of only four basic chemical units which are given the letters A, G, C and T.

There are over 3000 million letters in the DNA of every single cell. That's more letters than there are in ten Encyclopaedia Brittanicas! (So the words 'Tag' and 'Cat' appear quite a lot.)

The DNA has to be very tightly packed to fit into the nucleus, but stretched out, the DNA from a single cell would measure more than 1.5 metres in length.

A single DNA strand can have any sequence of the four letters. Here's a random bit of DNA sequence:

AATCGTAATTCGGC

Given the sequence on one strand, we know straight away what the sequence of chemical units will be on the other *(complementary)* strand because A and T, like G and C, are 'molecular mates'. Wherever A occurs in the DNA molecule, it is always paired up with T, and wherever G occurs, it is always paired up with C. These pairs form the 'stairs' of the DNA spiral staircase.

But if DNA is a code. what is it a code for?

DNA codes for proteins - chemical building blocks which create the structure and form of living things.

T
C
G
C
T
A
C
G

too many enzymes for tea!

For example, keratin is the protein found in hair and skin, haemoglobin in blood, and collagen in ligaments and cartilage. Proteins can also be **enzymes** - biological catalysts which speed up chemical reactions in the body.

Without proteins you'd just be a pool of sticky liquid on the floor.

Say, buddy can you spare a protein?

One of the questions which puzzled scientists for years was how DNA, a language with only four letters, codes for the thousands of different proteins in a human. Proteins are made up of chains of simpler chemical units called **amino acids**, which come in 20 different varieties. We now know that a gene is a string of three letter 'words', each word coding for a single amino acid.

DNA is "unzipped" and the code is copied by a messenger

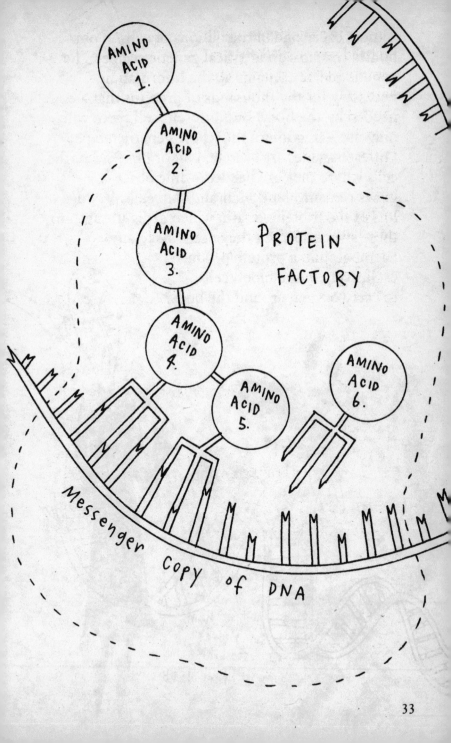

AMINO ACID 1.

AMINO ACID 2.

AMINO ACID 3.

PROTEIN FACTORY

AMINO ACID 4.

AMINO ACID 5.

AMINO ACID 6.

Messenger copy of DNA

Almost every one of the billions of cells in our bodies contains an identical genetic recipe. The genetic recipe contains all the information necessary for the thousands of proteins that are needed by the body. But different cell types will only use a fraction of the whole genetic recipe. Different genes are switched on or *expressed* in the cells where they are needed, while other genes remain silent. Hair and skin cells produce lots of the protein keratin which gives strength to these structures, but they don't make any haemoglobin, a protein produced exclusively in the blood cells to carry oxygen around the body.

OOPS

RVB

Look here baldy. Blood does not contain keratin, it's in the hair. So there's no use biting my bum to find it. Ok?

If you compare the sequence of A, T, C and G on one chromosome with the sequence on its partner chromosome, there are parts where they are identical, but in other parts they seem a bit different. What's going on?

Look at this, this is interesting! Let's stretch the chromosomes out a bit so that we can see the letters more easily

≲GLUB≲ — help.

BLUE EYES

BROWN EYES

HAZEL EYES

Genes, like chromosomes, come in pairs. Each pair of chromosomes carries two copies of a gene, one copy on each chromosome. But the two genes in a pair are not always exact replicas of one another. Although they will both shape the same characteristic - giving colour to your eyes for example - they may code for slightly different versions of a protein.

BLACK + WHITE STRIPED EYES (contact lenses)

This is why there is variation within a characteristic from one person to another - different hair and eye colours, for example, and the whole range of physical characteristics involved in how we look. Your eye colour genes specify the precise colour of your eyes.

This difference in the genes on partner chromosomes is known as *genetic variation*. Without the potential for this variation, humans would have ended up as identical copies of each other!
(If humans evolved at all - see page 52.)

And now to sex

Every gene pair on your chromosomes is
made up of one copy from your mother
and one copy from your father. You are a
mixture of half your mother's genes and
half your father's. Sex is not just about
reproduction, it's also for mixing genes!

We all start life as a single cell, produced by an
egg cell from your mother fusing with a sperm
cell from your father: **fertilization**, in
biological language. The sex cells - the eggs and
sperm - are unlike all other cells in the body.
They only carry 23 chromosomes - half the
normal number.

HOOEE

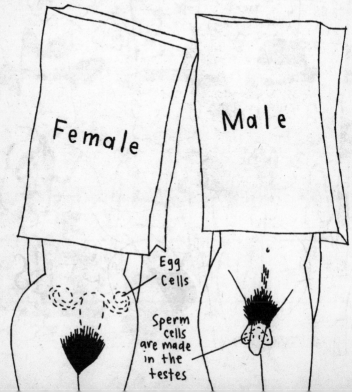

Female

Male

Egg
Cells

Sperm
cells
are made
in the
testes

Why do the sex cells only have 23 chromosomes? Well, think about what would happen if they had 46 instead. When a sperm cell fused with an egg, the total number of chromosomes would be 46 + 46 = 92. The number of chromosomes would be doubled each generation, and there'd soon be no room in the cells for anything else!

and finding a jersey to fit is a nightmare.

Having only 23 chromosomes ensures that when a sperm and egg fuse together we get back to the original number of chromosomes: 23 + 23 = 46.

eX

Sells

The sex cells come about through a special type of cell division called **meiosis** which halves the number of chromosomes.

The partners in each pair of chromosomes line up together

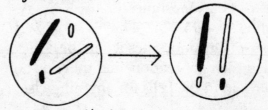

and then shuffle their genes with one another to create a completely new genetic mixture

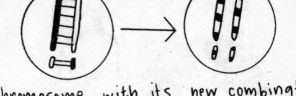

Each chromosome, with its new combination of genes, pulls away from its partner to the opposite end of the cell,

before the cell divides into two.

POP

So the sex cells are like little information packets carrying a random sample of half your genes. Which bits of information you receive from your mother and father will determine whether you're a boy or a girl, have blue or brown eyes, dark or fair hair, or any of the other thousands of characteristics which distinguish you from everyone else. Sexual reproduction is just a genetic lottery!

Once a sperm has fused with an egg to form the first cell of a new life, the single cell, or **embryo**, starts to grow and divide.

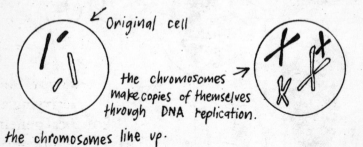

One cell becomes two cells
two cells become four cells
four cells become eight cells...

This cell division is called **mitosis**. Unlike meiosis, the number of chromosomes stays the same with each cell division. This can only be achieved through DNA's amazing ability to make copies of itself. Before a cell divides, all 46 chromosomes make a copy of themselves, so that each new cell carries an identical set of genes.

Original cell

the chromosomes make copies of themselves through DNA replication.

the chromosomes line up.

and then the chromosomes pull away from each other to opposite ends of the cell.

before the cell divides in two →

PoP

As the cells continue to divide, they begin to take on different roles - to form the different tissues that will eventually make up a fully developed body. Nobody is exactly sure how the cells do this; in fact it remains one of the great mysteries in biology. Remember that each cell is genetically identical. But somehow the cells manage to organize themselves into eyes, ears, heart, lungs and so on, using an incredibly complicated system of chemical communication.

But what about us?

Sometimes when a fertilized egg starts to divide, the two cells separate from one another and go on to divide and develop independently. This results in two embryos, each carrying an identical genetic recipe - identical twins. So identical twins will always be of the same sex. But the other sort of twins - fraternal twins - can be of either sex.

Fraternal twins come about when two eggs are released from the ovaries and each one is fertilized by a different sperm.

Accidents will happen

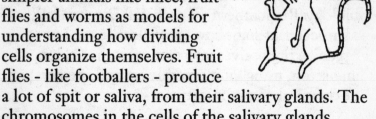

How dare you call me simple. I have a PhD you know.

Because human beings are so complicated, scientists use much simpler animals like mice, fruit flies and worms as models for understanding how dividing cells organize themselves. Fruit flies - like footballers - produce a lot of spit or saliva, from their salivary glands. The chromosomes in the cells of the salivary glands (fruit flies', not footballers') are unusually large, and there are only 4 pairs, so they're much easier to study than the chromosomes of other animals (and see page 66).

Funnily enough, one of the best ways of understanding how things work is by looking at what happens when things go wrong. Sometimes fruit flies develop which have bits of their bodies in the wrong place - they might have legs on their heads, or eyes on their legs!

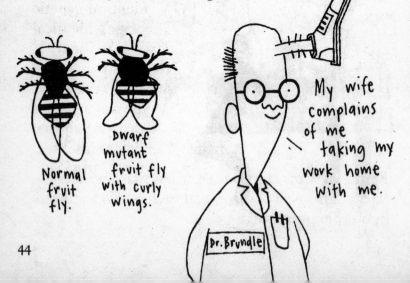

Normal fruit fly.

Dwarf mutant fruit fly with curly wings.

My wife complains of me taking my work home with me.

Dr. Brundle

These weird changes are caused by **mutations** - genetic accidents. As cells divide, the genetic message is not always transmitted in its original form. Sometimes mistakes are made. It's a bit like a biological version of Chinese whispers. Genetic accidents are going on all the time. In fact, it's almost certain that some bit of your DNA has changed since you started reading this book. Thankfully, not all mutations have such drastic effects as those seen in some of the fruit flies!

2 hours later

At least now I don't have to do Gym class.

A mutation can be a change in a single letter of the DNA, or it can mean blocks of letters being deleted or moved from one part of the DNA to another. Imagine the DNA letter sequence being like a sentence in the English language and see how mutations can affect DNA. The original letter sequence making up the sentence is:

The cat sat on the mat

Some mutations have little effect on the meaning of the DNA code:

The cat sat on the mat → The Kat sat on the mat

Others can change the meaning altogether:

The cat sat on the mat → The hat sat on the mat

While others can make the message nonsensical:

The cat sat on the mat → The eat sat on the mat

And others change the whole sequence:

The mat cat the sat on

- the cat is unhappy

Mutations occur naturally. In fact, mutations explain why we grow old and die. As time goes by, more and more mistakes pile up in our genetic recipes until eventually, the cell machinery which keeps us ticking over becomes crippled beyond repair.

But mutations can also be triggered by chemicals in the environment or by radiation. It's a grim statistic, but about one in every four people on the planet will die of some form of cancer. Most cancers are caused by mutations in genes which then change the normal behaviour of cells in the body.

Smoking and ultra-violet light from the sun can trigger mutations - so both will increase your chances of getting cancer.

Causes of cancer

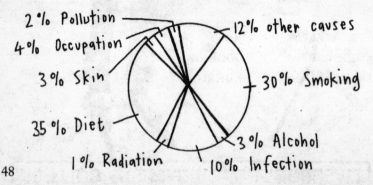

Following the massive explosion at the Chernobyl nuclear power station in 1986, radioactive dust rained down on the countryside for miles around. This was bad news for anyone living nearby. Their genes took a hammering from the massive doses of radiation which they were exposed to. Not surprisingly, the incidence of cancer amongst the people who were exposed to the radiation has shot up over the last ten years.

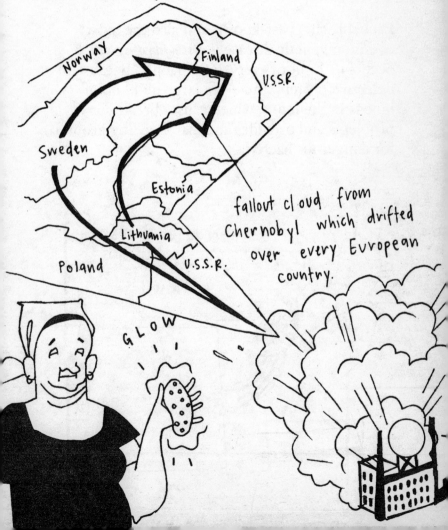

fallout cloud from Chernobyl which drifted over every European country.

Genetic diseases are diseases caused by mutations in a normal working copy of a gene: that is, they're caused by something inside the cells, rather than by infection from outside, as in a bacterial or viral disease. About 5000 different genetic diseases have been identified in humans so far. The genes responsible for these diseases either produce a defective version of the normal protein, or no protein at all.

Probably the best-known and also the most common genetic disease is *cystic fibrosis*, which occurs in 1 out of every 2500 people. Because of a defective protein, there is a large build up of mucus in the lungs, which causes breathing problems and provides an ideal breeding ground for dangerous bacteria.

Genetic accidents can also extend to the whole chromosome. Sometimes, when the sex cells are being made, the chromosome pairs don't separate from one another properly, so that some of the sex cells have an extra copy of one of the 23 chromosomes. If one of these cells is fertilized by a normal sex cell, every cell in the body will end up carrying the extra chromosome. People with Down's syndrome have 47 chromosomes instead of the normal 46.

An extra chromosome.

But although messing with a well worked genetic recipe is often harmful, there are times when a genetic change will match or even improve on what's gone before. The genetic differences we see between ourselves and between other creatures have all come about through mutation at some time in the past.

without mutations there would be no variety.

Without variety there would be no evolution.

it's the new "look"

without evolution you wouldn't be sitting reading this book!

- help.

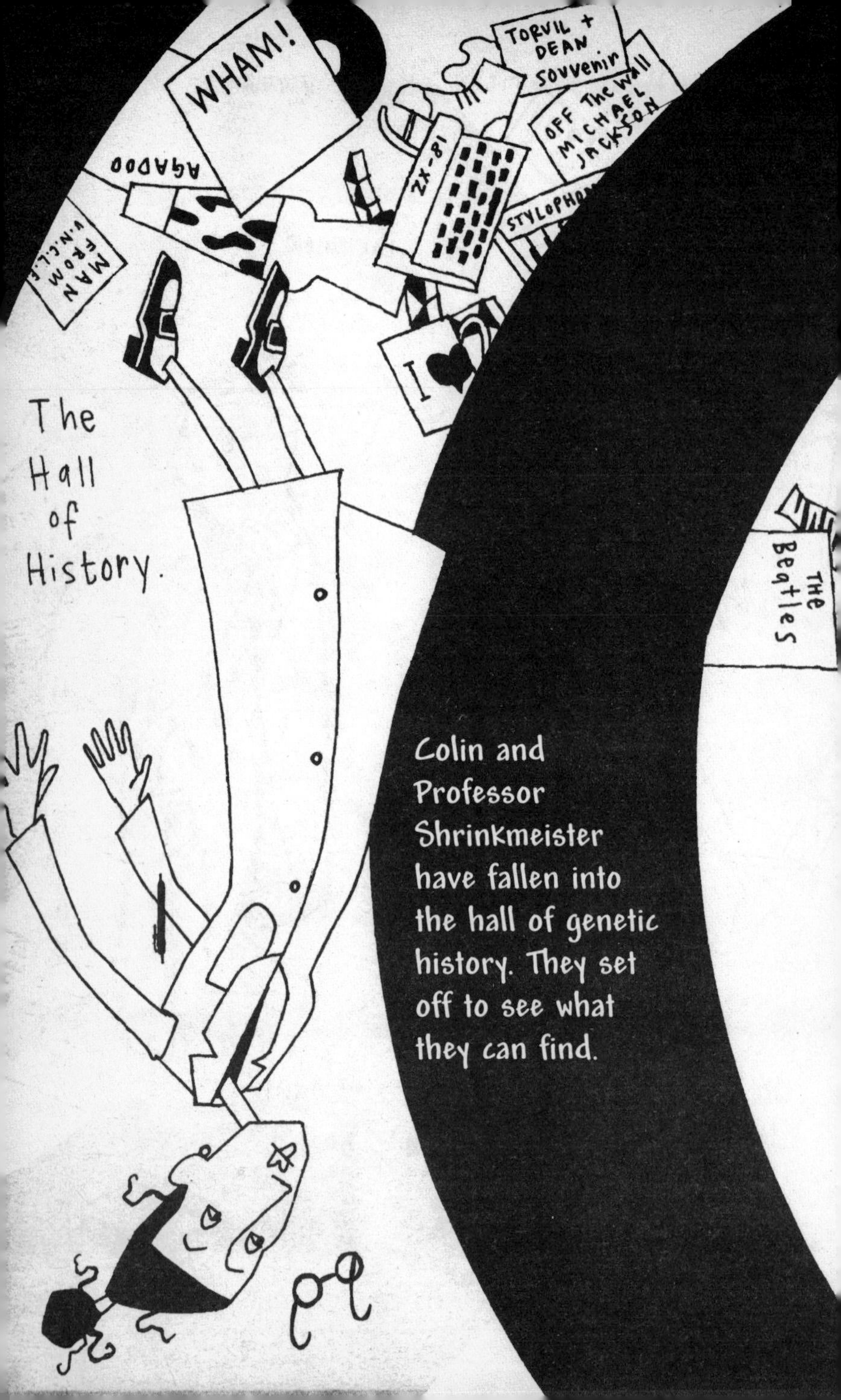

WHAM!

TORVIL +
DEAN
SOUVENIR

OFF THE WALL
MICHAEL
JACKSON

AGADOO

ZX-81

STYLOPHONE

MAN
FROM
U.N.C.L.E

I ❤

THE
Beatles

The
Hall
of
History.

Colin and
Professor
Shrinkmeister
have fallen into
the hall of genetic
history. They set
off to see what
they can find.

For thousands of years people didn't have much of a clue about the way in which physical characteristics were passed on from parents to their children - inheritance was all a bit of a mystery.

Some thought that inheritance was like the mixing of paints, that a child was a blend of its parent's characteristics.

But children are not always something midway between their parents. Sometimes a characteristic in one parent will disappear in their children, only to reappear in their grandchildren.

How could this be?

The answer came from the study of pea plants, not of humans. An Austrian monk called **Gregor Mendel** was fascinated by the inheritance of characteristics in pea plants which he bred in his monastery garden. Mendel used two strains of plant which were both *pure breeding* - the offspring always looked like their parents - and which differed from one another in only a single characteristic, pea shape. One strain had round peas, the other wrinkled peas.

When a plant with round peas was mated to one with wrinkled peas, all the offspring had round peas. But when these round pea plants were mated together, they produced both types of offspring. The wrinkled characteristic had disappeared in one generation and reappeared in the next. But the other strange thing was that round and wrinkled peas were not produced in equal proportions. There were always about three round peas to every wrinkled one.

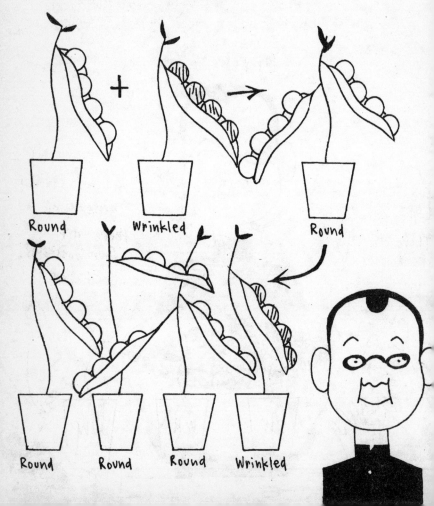

Round   Wrinkled   Round

Round   Round   Round   Wrinkled

Mendel had a brainwave. He realized that his results could be explained if pea shape was coded by a pair of factors (what we now call genes), which separate from one another during the formation of either male sex cells (pollen, in plants) or eggs.

It's easiest to think of the genes in terms of symbols, **R** for **R**ound and **W** for **W**rinkled. Pure-breeding round pea plants carry two copies of the R gene - their **genotype** is RR. Likewise the genotype of pure-breeding wrinkled peas is WW.

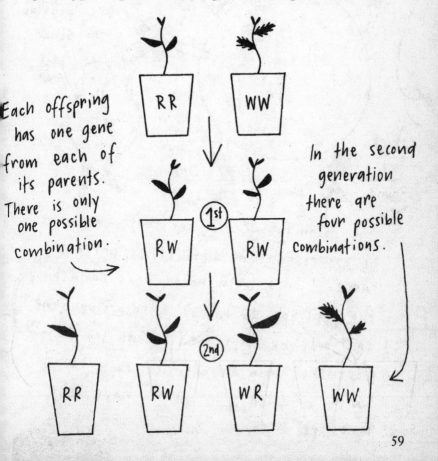

Each offspring has one gene from each of its parents. There is only one possible combination.

In the second generation there are four possible combinations.

All the offspring of a mating between pure breeding round and wrinkled plants will have the genotype RW because they will all get an R gene from one parent and a W gene from the other. But although these plants carry two different genes, their peas are round. The gene for round peas masks the gene for wrinkled peas. R is **dominant** to the **recessive** W gene.

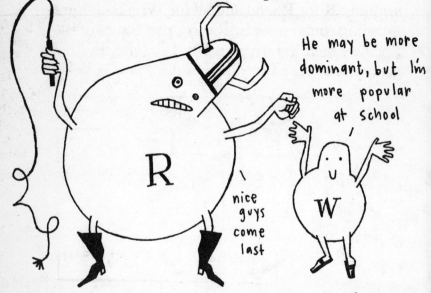

He may be more dominant, but I'm more popular at school

nice guys come last

A dominant gene is one that will always be expressed regardless of its partner gene. Plants with round peas could have the genotype RR or RW. A recessive gene can only be expressed when it's partnered with an identical copy. Plants with wrinkled peas must have the genotype WW.

But what happens when two of these RW round plants are mated together? The offspring could get either an R or a W gene from either parent. Mendel realized that which of the two gene copies is inherited from each parent is a game of chance, just like tossing a coin and seeing if it falls heads or tails.

Possible combinations:

toss a COIN not a COLIN.

		Gene from Parent 1.	
		R or	W
Gene from Parent 2.	R or W	RR round	RW round
		RW Round	WW wrinkled

So on average amongst the offspring, you would expect to see three round pea plants produced for every wrinkled pea plant.

what have I started?

Because of his work, Mendel is regarded as the founding father of genetics, despite the fact that he failed his science exams at university! But Mendel's work was ignored until long after his death, and only at the beginning of the 20th century did people begin to recognize its importance.

We now know that hundreds of human characteristics, and many genetic diseases, are inherited in an identical way to the shape of Mendel's peas.

Na Na N.
told
you so
smarty
pants
professor!

Cystic fibrosis is a recessive genetic disease - only people with two copies of the cystic fibrosis gene will actually get the disease. The disease affects about one in 2500 people, but about one in 20 people carry one copy of the gene. Although they don't have the disease, they are known as *carriers*. All of us carry recessive genes in our genetic recipes that would make us ill or even kill us if we had two copies of the gene instead of just the one.

However, the appearance of such lethal recipes depends on two carriers meeting *and* the two recessive genes both being passed on to their offspring.

Imagine that two people decide to have a child. But they're shocked to discover, through genetic testing (see page 92), that they are both carriers for cystic fibrosis. What's the chance that their first child would have the disease? (Clue: it's exactly the same as the chance of getting a wrinkled pea plant from a mating between two round (RW) plants).

The child would have a 1 in 4 chance of having the disease.

Jane has ambitions to be a game show host.

Brad feels he is a woman trapped in a man's body.

Angela will change the way we think of cheese in the future.

Louise will become a great body builder.

4 POSSIBILITIES

Have you ever wondered where the legend of the werewolf comes from? Genetics may have the answer.

my auntie Gladys

People who suffer from the genetic disease *porphyria* are unable to make the red pigment in the blood. They are also very sensitive to light (the effects of a full moon?) and in extreme cases, hair may grow on exposed skin. They also produce urine which is blood-red in colour, and often suffer from bouts of madness. In fact, it's possible that the famously mad King George III of England suffered from the disease.

Unlike cystic fibrosis, porphyria is a dominant genetic disease - you only need one copy of the porphyria gene to be affected. In the rare event that someone inherits two copies of the gene, the disease will almost certainly kill them.

RIGHT TREATMENT

"you won't feel a thing."

tippy toe

KILL KILL the EVIL ONE / Yahoo

WRONG TREATMENT

I have a silver bullet -

Oh no!
It's T.H.
Morgan
and his
fruit
flies!

By the start of the
twentieth century
geneticists had
moved from peas to
flies. Because genetics is
a game of chance, scientists realized that you
needed lots of offspring to work out the rules of
inheritance. Fruit flies - like peas - produce lots of
offspring, but they also have a much shorter life
cycle. In about two weeks, a fertilized fruit fly egg
can grow into an adult fly which is ready to
reproduce in turn. In comparison, humans take
about 20 years! What you could achieve in a
year working on fruit flies would take 500 years
in humans!

look, I'm terribly sorry
but my great uncle
Wilfrid seems
to have made
a mistake
about 300 years
ago and I'm
afraid we will have
to start the
experiment over
again.

T.H. Morgan's claim to fame was discovering where genes were located. Morgan was working with two strains of fruit fly. One had red eyes and the other had white eyes. In his breeding experiments, Morgan noticed that males always had the same coloured eyes as their mother. If the mother had red eyes, all her sons had red eyes. If she had white eyes, then her sons would also have white eyes. The colour of the father's eyes made no difference.

In fruit flies, like humans, females have two X chromosomes and males have an X and a Y chromosome. Because males always inherit their X chromosome from their mother, Morgan reasoned that the only way to explain his results was if the gene for eye colour was carried on the X chromosome.

Genes were on chromosomes!

Yaa Hoo!

In humans, the stubby Y chromosome carries the gene which makes an egg develop into a male, but little else. This is bad news for males. Any gene - whether dominant or recessive - on the X chromosome will always be expressed because it has no partner gene.

The genes which cause red-green colour blindness and haemophilia are both found on the X chromosome. If a male inherits only one copy of the recessive gene, he will have the disease, whereas a female has to inherit two. Not surprisingly, both these conditions are much more common in males than females.

X Y

People with haemophilia are unable to make a vital blood clotting factor, so that they bleed very heavily from even the slightest wound.
Haemophilia is often called a disease of royalty because all of Queen Victoria's sons suffered from it. The queen herself was unaffected. She only carried a single copy of the gene whose effects were masked by the normal dominant gene on her other X chromosome.

Mam I cut myself shaving again.

≥ sigh ≥
if only we had electric razors.

It was the English scientist **Archibald Garrod**
who discovered a link between genes and proteins.
Garrod was studying an inherited genetic disease
called alkaptonuria. He found that people with the
disease lacked a crucial enzyme and this caused
their urine to turn black when exposed to air!
GENES MAKE PROTEINS!

Meanwhile, what genes were made of was still a bit of a mystery. Scientists knew about DNA, but they thought that it was far too simple a molecule to be the genetic material. Most scientists believed that proteins were the only molecules complex enough to store genetic information.

71

But opinions soon changed after some experiments on *viruses*. Viruses are tiny particles, which spend their entire lives making a nuisance of themselves inside other organisms. Many diseases in humans and other animals, and also plants, are caused by viruses. They include things like measles, mumps, chickenpox, influenza, rabies, herpes and AIDS. If a dog is man's best friend, then a virus must be man's worst enemy.

In 1952, **Alfred Hershey** and **Martha Chase** were working on *bacteriophages* - viruses which infect bacteria. (A bacteriophage is just a bit of DNA encased in a protein shell.)

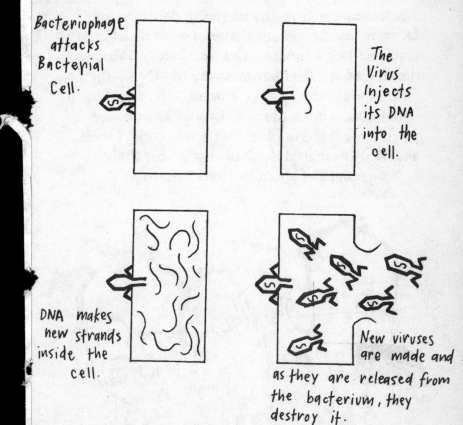

Bacteriophage attacks Bacterial Cell.

The Virus Injects its DNA into the cell.

DNA makes new strands inside the cell.

New viruses are made and as they are released from the bacterium, they destroy it.

When bacteriophages reproduce, they inject only their DNA into the bacterial cell, *leaving the protein coat behind.* The DNA then makes new virus particles inside the cell. This provided the strongest evidence yet that DNA *is* the genetic material.

The following year, any lingering doubts about DNA being the genetic material were finally put to rest. In 1953, **Francis Crick** and **James Watson** discovered the detailed structure of DNA - the DNA spiral staircase! Its structure revealed how it could make copies of itself through the unique pairing mechanism of its four-letter code. Crick and Watson shared the Nobel prize for their amazing piece of chemical detective work.

Wow! I didn't realize genetics
had advanced so quickly. Only a few
pages ago we were in among
the pea plants of an Austrian monk
and now we're looking at the
genetic code itself!

It is impressive. But since 1953, things have
moved even faster. You should see what's going on
in genetics today. Genetics is BIG science, and
there's a whole new technology that's affecting our
lives in a way we could never have imagined forty
years ago. And the key to it all was the discovery
of DNA as the genetic code.

The clone zone

Genetics today often resembles advanced cookery, with DNA as the main ingredient. The laboratory has become the geneticist's kitchen, complete with test tubes and expensive gadgets. It's now a fairly routine business to pull out the DNA from cells, cut it up, splice it back together again, and do all sorts of other fiddly little things with it.

Allo.
Tooday on ma wurld of genetic cookery we weel make a garlic flavoured onion to save on ma wasteeing ma time trying to teach you 'opeless mushy pea and spud peeple 'ow to cook.

Woman.
by Dr. Dork

hoo-ee

hooray!

Hey!

I don't think so

As you can see my proposal is to create a woman who will only be attracted to balding short sighted boffins

PROF. DORK

Scientists can stick a bit of DNA into one end of a machine and get its complete sequence of letters out of the other.

Using chemical trickery, we can copy individual genes many millions of times in a test tube, and then put them into cells where they might not normally be. Scientists can create new and unique recipes by mixing up the genetic ingredients - they can even engineer new life forms.

the Womnip.
(½ Parsnip ½ Wombat)

for vegetarian hunters →

Genetic engineering is a way of creating life forms with new combinations of genes designed to suit human needs.

Genetic engineering in five easy steps!

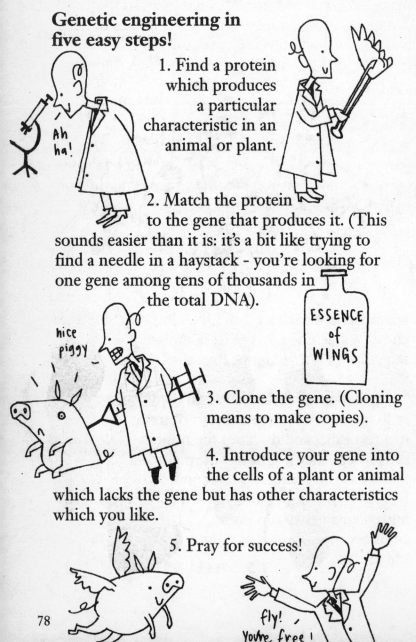

1. Find a protein which produces a particular characteristic in an animal or plant.

2. Match the protein to the gene that produces it. (This sounds easier than it is: it's a bit like trying to find a needle in a haystack - you're looking for one gene among tens of thousands in the total DNA).

Ah ha!

nice piggy

ESSENCE of WINGS

3. Clone the gene. (Cloning means to make copies).

4. Introduce your gene into the cells of a plant or animal which lacks the gene but has other characteristics which you like.

5. Pray for success!

fly! you're free!

Genetic engineering first hit the headlines when it was used to produce human insulin for people suffering from diabetes. Diabetics are unable to make sufficient insulin for themselves, so the protein has to be injected into their bodies to keep their blood sugar levels under control. The injected insulin used to come from other animals, but many diabetics became allergic to animal insulin. So scientists put the normal insulin gene into a strain of bacteria. The human gene is incorporated into the bacterial DNA to become a part of its new genetic recipe. These bacteria have become human insulin factories, producing lots of human insulin as they grow.

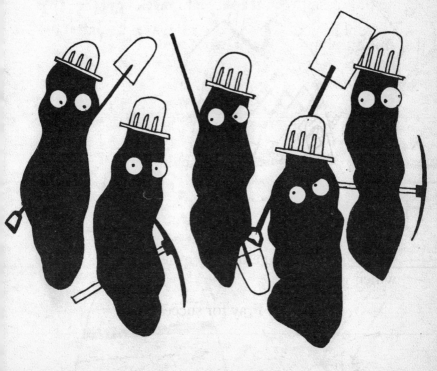

Haemophiliacs have also benefited from genetic engineering. Remember that people who suffer from haemophilia are unable to make a protein which is needed for normal blood clotting. They have to get the protein from regular blood transfusions. But blood is always in short supply, so genetic engineers decided to clone the gene for the blood clotting protein and put it into the DNA of a sheep. The sheep, with its new bit of human DNA, produces lots of the protein in its milk. The protein can be easily purified from the milk and then injected into haemophiliacs who need it.

Yes! Same thing happened to me after those shots. I much prefer the Argyll pattern.

Human heart transplants are now fairly routine operations. Unfortunately, the demand for new hearts far exceeds the supply. There just aren't enough donors. However, because pig hearts are remarkably similar to those of humans, a pig's heart could probably do the job just as well. But if you put a pig's heart inside a human being, the body will recognize the heart as foreign and reject it. Proteins on the surface of the pig's heart cells give the game away. So geneticists have got round the problem by inserting genes, which make the equivalent proteins in humans, into the pig's genetic recipe. The cell surface proteins trick the body into 'thinking' that the heart is human.

Transplanting pig hearts into humans is now possible, but won't be done using genetically-engineered hearts until other safety aspects have been tested. People are worried about the possibility of introducing new diseases - from pigs - into humans. In the light of the BSE ('mad cow disease') crisis, where a disease spread from cows to humans through the eating of infected meat, these are understandable worries.

SPAMELA HAMDERSON

SNORT
GUZZLE

` Ever since
that operation
you eat like a
pig

GRUNT

A feast of genes?

If you're munching away as you read this book, it's possible that the food you've just put into your mouth has been genetically engineered in some way. Such food is already on the supermarket shelves, and all the signs are that there'll be much more to come in the future. One of the latest products is genetically modified soya beans, used in bread, cakes, margarine, and most processed food.

Not Again!
Doltish
child.

Genetically
Engineered
BEANS

I swopped
it for our
cloned
cow.

← JACK

STUMBLE

What's so special about this Soya stuff?

Scientists discovered a gene in a species of bacteria which made it resistant to weed killer.

The gene was isolated and put in amongst the soya plant's own DNA so that the soya plant, with its new bit of foreign DNA, was made resistant to the weed killer.

Using the genetically engineered plant helps farmers improve their harvest because they can now spray weed killer on the crops all year round without worrying about killing the soya plants.

As long as the weed killer doesn't kill everything else too...

There are hundreds more genetically engineered food products currently being developed. Not everyone is happy with the idea of genetically-engineered food, and some people say that the risks are greater than the benefits.

When you have finished painting the dining room, go and give the cows a hand milking themselves

Crossing a sheep with an odd job man was one of the best things I ever did.

OK B

Take the soya for example. Who benefits from the production of these new, engineered, crops? In one sense we all do. Certainly, the companies which come up with the new crops make money by selling them to the farmer. The farmer also stands to make more money by improving the harvest. And an increased supply of food might also benefit you and me, the consumers, by lowering food prices in the shops.

But other people are concerned about the possible environmental impact of these genetically-engineered plants. They argue that plants made resistant to weedkillers might breed with the wild relatives of the soya to create new varieties of superweeds - potentially resistant to all man-made weed killers. These superweeds would spread like wildfire through the countryside, taking over from rarer plants which would become extinct.

FREEZE!
WEED
POLICE.

this is
harassment.
just because
I'm not
a tulip.

However, some of the newly engineered agricultural products might help the environment. Fruit and vegetables have already been designed that are resistant to insect pests and certain types of disease, and so one day, environmentally dangerous chemicals like pesticides may be unnecessary.

hopefully this will one day lead to pre-salted pop corn.

One particular example is a potato which has been genetically engineered to commit suicide when it is infected by a disease-causing fungus. The suicidal potato has a special bacterial gene incorporated into its genetic recipe. This gene makes a very aggressive kind of protein which stops the production of all other proteins in the potato's cells and so eventually kills it. But the gene is only switched on when the fungus attacks. The potato dies, but in a field of potatoes this is good news, because the disease is prevented from spreading - without the need for pesticides.

Grab air

Maybe preservatives could also disappear if we could design food which didn't go off. Far-fetched? Maybe not. Supermarkets are now selling a brand of tomato puree which uses tomatoes made resistant to bruising through genetic engineering.

URRGH

It might sound too good to be true. Indeed, there are fears that by creating super-resistant crops, the disease-causing organisms might one day mutate to overcome these new obstacles and become even more dangerous than they were to start with.

Could genetically-engineered food help the hungry? In places like India and Pakistan, much of the soil is too salty to grow crops. But it might be possible to put a gene from a native salt-loving plant into a food crop like wheat, so that it could be grown in salty soils. Again, this sounds like a good idea. But environmental organizations like Greenpeace have argued that poverty, not lack of food, is the reason why people are starving in the Third World. Are the claims made by genetic engineering companies just propaganda?

hooray

Manipulating individual genes can have unpredictable consequences because genes often work together as a team. Like the transfer of a star player between football teams, genetic engineering does not always guarantee success. The food might look good but taste bad. Or it might taste great but have little nutritional value. It might even cause you to have a bad reaction, if the manipulated gene has conspired with its new genetic neighbours to produce an unexpected and allergy-causing chemical.

I bought some fruit that had "gone bad" not knowing what the shop really meant.

I'll show you soup

Perhaps some of the fear surrounding genetically engineered food also reflects a more general fear of new technology. Many of those who are opposed to it say that we shouldn't be tampering with nature. But humans have been tampering with nature for thousands of years. Pigs, sheep, cows, Brussels sprouts - none of these would exist without the long history of human interference in nature.

Selective breeding of plants and animals and genetic engineering both have the same aim - producing plants and animals which are adapted to the needs of humans rather than those of nature. There's already talk of engineering a square tomato and a straight banana. It might seem trivial, but if it makes the packaging of the fruit more efficient then why not?

You know, after I ate that synthetic parsnip, my mind has cleared up enormously. I feel so much more positive about being called 'a rat!'

From genes to revelations

Genetic technology has many uses apart from engineering new life forms. It is widely used in *prenatal diagnosis* - checking whether a foetus is healthy before it is born. From a few cells taken from a growing foetus, doctors can obtain all sorts of information about it, and detect any abnormal signs. The chromosomes can be looked at under a microscope to determine the sex of the child and to check that each cell contains the normal 23 pairs. The DNA can be removed from the cells and screened for disease-causing genes. At the moment, tests exist for only a few genetic diseases, but the list continues to grow.

By uncovering any potential problems at an early stage, prenatal diagnosis can help parents plan ahead. Although no cure has yet been found for any genetic disease, sometimes the symptoms of the disease can be treated.

People with haemophilia, for example, lack a vital blood clotting protein. But they can live perfectly normal lives providing they are given regular doses of the protein.

Other genetic diseases cause terrible physical pain and suffering for the person who is affected, and emotional pain for their parents. If a genetic test reveals that a child is destined to have a short and painful life, the parents may consider abortion as the most humane option.

Genetic tests can also prepare prospective parents for future possibilities, if they decide to have a child. From a small sample of blood, or a simple mouth swab, our own genetic recipes can be screened to see if they contain genes which cause disease.

Genetic counsellors are trained to understand the results of genetic tests and to educate people about genetic diseases, to help them understand the risks for their children.

Tay-Sachs syndrome is a very unpleasant recessive disease which kills children before they're five. If two prospective parents are tested and found to be carriers for the disease, their child will have a one in four chance of having Tay-Sachs.

The disease is unusually common among people from orthodox Jewish society. Arranged marriages are still practised in these communities, and the results of a genetic test can affect whether partners are considered suitable for one another.

You match too well. You can't get married

There are now alternative forms of pre-natal diagnosis which happen at a stage which can avoid abortion. *Pre-implantation diagnosis* screens the embryo before it attaches itself to the mother's womb. This is only done when an egg is fertilized *outside* the mother's body - that is, *in vitro* fertilization.

Nearly right.

try again.

A cell is taken from the three day old embryo, which is still only a ball of cells at this stage, and its genetic recipe is screened. If it is healthy, then the embryo can be put into the mother's womb to develop and grow as normal.

Because unhealthy embryos are discarded, pre-implantation diagnosis is still morally unacceptable to some people, and in certain countries, the technique is illegal. In the UK, pre-implantation diagnosis is usually only recommended in cases where a family shows a history of inherited disease.

Sometimes people would rather not find out what their genes might have in store for them. This is particularly true for diseases like *Huntingdon's chorea*, which don't affect people until much later in life. People with Huntingdon's chorea appear perfectly normal until about middle age when their nervous system suddenly starts to break down. It's caused by a dominant gene - if you have one copy it will kill you once it becomes active. If a person finds out that one of their parents is affected by the disease, they face an awful dilemma. They know that they will have a fifty-fifty chance of having the gene. If they already have children, they may already have passed on the gene - but knowing their genetic make-up may prevent the gene being passed on any further. Do they reveal their fate by having the genetic test for the disease or do they remain in the dark and trust to luck?

How long will it be before we can cure a genetic disease? After all, if you can replace a defective organ, like a heart or kidney, why not replace a defective gene with a normal working copy?

Although genetic engineers insert new genes into the fertilized eggs of other animals and plants, scientists aren't allowed to tamper with the genetic recipes of human embryos. Any gene which is inserted into a fertilized egg will become part of the new genetic recipe in every cell of the body, including the sex cells, and will be passed on to future generations. This is too close to the image of designer babies - and eugenics (see page 21) - for most people's tastes.

Urrrr

Excuse me. I bought this child here a few years ago but it has not grown up to be fashionable enough. Can I have a new one.

Maw...

Certainly madam.

SHAKE

So instead, scientists are researching into the possibility of introducing working copies of defective genes into a person's cells which are most affected by the disease. This new science of **gene therapy** is still in its infancy, but there have already been some encouraging results in the treatment of cystic fibrosis sufferers. Because this is a disease which mainly affects the lungs, it might be possible to use a kind of inhaler to spray copies of the normal genes into the lungs, where they will be taken up by the lung cells.

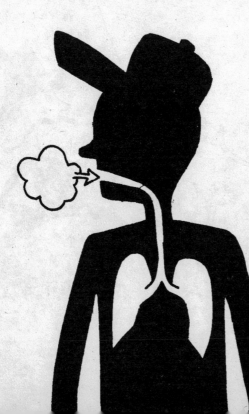

Gene therapy may one day be used in the treatment of cancer. One of the problems of treating cancers is that the drugs used kill not only the cancer cells, they also kill the healthy cells around the tumour, making patients feel extremely ill. But these unpleasant side effects might be reduced by inserting a newly developed gene into the DNA of the healthy cells, which can produce a protein to protect them from the dangerous effects of chemotherapy drugs.

Genetic testing and genetic engineering seem to offer many new and exciting medical benefits. But they also raise many moral questions about just how far science - in the hands of people - should go. Modern genetics is presenting us with choices and decisions which we have never had to make before. Should we allow a genetic test to decide the fate of an embryo? And which diseases should be screened for? All, or just the most serious ones? Who should decide a test should be done: the individual, the doctor, the state? When does a human life begin? At fertilization, after 3 weeks?

Different countries have their own laws on what is and what is not acceptable in genetics and genetics research. In the UK for instance, human embryos can only be used for research purposes up until they are 14 days old. In other countries, all human embryo research is banned. Some countries, like France, permit abortion, but do not allow pre-implantation diagnosis. This variety of national legislation partly reflects religious and cultural differences between different countries. But it might also reflect the moral confusion which modern genetics has introduced into our lives.

Criminal genes

You may be wondering where Colin and the Professor have got to. Well, they've been arrested on suspicion of stealing some of the DNA double helix from page 28. Although no-one saw them take it, they unwittingly left behind some vital clues. The police found a few strands of hair at the scene of the crime and they are keen to do some genetic tests on their two main suspects.

Genetic recipes are like thumbprints - no two are alike. Criminals don't just leave their thumbprints at the scene of a crime. They also leave behind hair, blood, saliva or skin, all containing copies of their unique genetic recipe - a genetic fingerprint, which the police can use to solve crimes. Our two culprits were arrested because the police found that their genetic fingerprints matched those found in the hairs on page 28!

We ken all aboot it Sonny Boy

In the future, genes might even be able to produce a photofit of a criminal. Scientists are building up a database containing the genetic recipes of a group of volunteers combined with photos of their faces, to see how well DNA predicts facial features. Perhaps one day it will be possible to analyse DNA from crime scenes and build up a photofit of the criminal by linking their likely physical features with their DNA codes.

Ah. P.C. Noggin. here is the DNA photofit from the samples we found at the zoo robbery.

The Human Genome Project

The Human **Genome** Project is the most ambitious scientific endeavour since the race to put a person on the Moon. The plan is to work out the entire sequence of DNA letters in a human being - all 3000 million of them! One person working every day of the year would take about ten thousand years to complete the task! Not surprisingly, the project has therefore been divided up between many

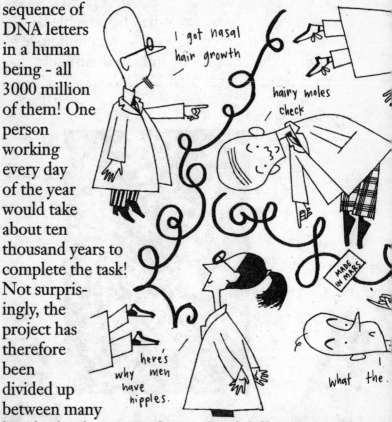

hundreds of scientists from several different countries, including Britain and the United States. They hope to finish around the year 2005.

The ultimate goal of the Human Genome Project is to make a complete genetic map of each of the 23 human chromosomes showing the positions of the 100,000 or so genes.

Meanwhile, scientists will begin the even more difficult task of working out exactly how each of these genes contributes to the day-to-day running of a normal human.

The project will cost hundreds of millions of pounds, and will involve a great deal of laborious and repetitive work. One of the problems is that a lot of the DNA in our cells doesn't seem to do anything at all. It doesn't code for proteins, or have any other known function, but just sits there taking up space on the chromosomes. As much as 90% of the total DNA in our cells may be junk. So scientists will have to spend a lot of time sifting through all this genetic nonsense.

From genes to eternity

For thousands of years, people have lived with the idea that their future was uncertain. You might live to be a hundred or you might die young of some horrible disease. You trust to luck, or God, perhaps. But knowledge about our genes is beginning to change all that.

tra la la life's all a game who knows what lies around the next corner.

OK Boys. here he comes.

Sometimes the message is clear: genes for diseases like cystic fibrosis and Huntingdon's chorea tell us what to expect if the defective genes aren't replaced. But scientists are now beginning to discover genes which carry a vaguer message. Such genes suggest that there may be a greater likelihood of a person getting breast or lung cancer, or having a heart attack, but development of these diseases will still be dependent on other factors - for example, what the person eats, how much exercise they take, whether they smoke.

These genes suggest the future, rather than predicting it with absolute certainty. Life is still a game of chance, but your genes can determine the odds.

≥ SIGH ≥ thanks to genetic advances I'm practically redundant now. The worst bit is, I didn't see it coming.

The question is, would you want to know what your own genes might have in store for you? Maybe you would, if you could do something about it. Recently, there was a case of a woman in Britain who had a genetic test which showed she had a high chance of getting breast cancer. There was a history of breast cancer in her family, and her own mother had died of it in middle age. Although she herself had no signs of the disease, she decided to have her breasts removed just to be on the safe side. She had used information about her own genetic recipe to protect herself for the future – but many people would think that the means of protection are too drastic to be worthwhile.

It's well known that smoking can cause lung cancer. But did you know that even if everyone smoked the same amount, we wouldn't all stand an equal risk of getting cancer? Genes which vary between people can also vary in their sensitivity to the damaging effects of cigarette smoke. If you knew your own genes, you might think even more carefully before taking up smoking.

We now know that our genes can affect many aspects of our lives. But what if our genes could also shape our personalities? Some scientists already believe that genes could have some influence on:

Whether we're straight or gay

Rasp

whether we are extroverted or introverted

whether we're likely to become criminals

our fondness for alcohol or drugs

The idea that we are helpless prisoners of our genes is pure science fiction. But as scientists continue to unravel the genetic code, there is a danger that the media, and even some scientists, are getting too preoccupied with genes and forgetting about all the other things that make us what we are. Who we are as people has as much to do with our family environment, and our social and cultural experiences, as it has to do with genes.

Leave me alone child. Daddy has important genetic experiments to carry out.

TUG TUG

Play with me I haven't seen you in four years

But because we're always trying to find easy answers to the problems of society, many people are attracted by the idea that some of us may be genetically programmed to become criminals, alcoholics or drug addicts. Even homelessness has been blamed on genes! It saves people having to think about the real reasons behind the problems in society, which are more complicated and require a lot more effort to put right. How much easier to blame everything on genes! But remember what happened the last time people thought too much about genes and not enough about society (see pages 20-23).

There are already signs that some people are keen to exercise their prejudices against those they consider abnormal. A few years ago, the newspapers reported the discovery of the 'gay gene', after a scientist found that there was a bit of DNA on the X chromosome that was shared by some gay men. *The Daily Mail* reported on the discovery with the headline 'Abortion hope after "gay genes" findings'.

The idea of choosing a child based on its genes isn't new. In India, parents who follow their traditions strictly prefer sons because daughters are more expensive - they need large dowries when they are eventually married off. In the past it was common for pregnant women to have abortions if a prenatal test diagnosed the foetus as female. India now has five men for every four women.

Maybe the range of choices open to parents in the future will be far greater than it is today. If scientists begin to identify the genes for the thousands of different human characteristics, will parents want to choose their child in the same way they'd choose a new car? Will children end up suing their parents for knowingly passing on defective genes to them, or for giving them genetic characteristics they don't like? And will people use knowledge about their own genetic recipes to assess the suitability of a prospective partner? Scientists are currently developing a "genetic chip" - a microscopic device that could one day screen thousands of genes in an afternoon. In theory, this would enable every person's genetic recipe to be screened. In the future, your genetic ID may sit alongside - or even replace - the photo in your passport.

Hello Dolly!

Unless you've been living on Mars, it will have been difficult for you to have avoided hearing about Dolly the sheep. Dolly is a very special sheep because she is the first-ever clone of an adult mammal. Dolly did not start life in the way that most animals do, through the fusion of a sperm and egg. Her entire genetic recipe came from one cell of a six year old sheep. This was a truly amazing scientific experiment, something which many people, scientists included, thought would never happen.

First a cell was taken from the udder of an adult sheep.

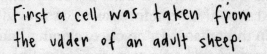

Then the chromosomes were taken out of the cell.

These chromosomes were then put into an empty egg cell (one which had had its own chromosomes removed).

The egg was then given an electric shock to jump start development.

And then the egg was put into the womb of a sheep.

Back again!

Where it continued to divide and grow until....

hello dolly!

When Dolly was announced to the world, the media went absolutely bananas. How long, they asked, would it be before scientists moved from sheep to humans? In practice, cloning humans would probably only require a bit of fine tuning. But people seem terrified at the prospect and research into human cloning has already been banned in the UK. Perhaps this fear is further evidence that society is thinking too much about genes. After all, we already have human clones in the form of identical twins. Just because people share identical genetic recipes doesn't mean they are the same person. Environment still has its part to play.

19th Annual Clone reunion

what do you do?

Anarchy

So what do you drive now? I have a fiesta.

a hog.

oin

There is a danger that cloning technology could be misused if it got into the wrong hands. Just because it's illegal it doesn't mean that someone somewhere in the world won't have a go at creating a human clone. Could human clones be used as factories for the growth and sale of human organs on the black market? Or perhaps cloning could create an entire winning team of 220 cm basketball players; or a fighting army of super strong men; or create a line of physically identical dictators?

one day sale

buy 3 and get one free.

I have thousands of money off coupons

I cloned this lady and with her super powers of thrift intend to deprive the world of bargains.

Von Boffin evil genius.

And how about using cloning technology to raise the dead? When people die, their DNA breaks down along with the rest of the body, as nature works the molecules of life back into the soil. But occasionally, dead bodies can be preserved. In fact, the ancient Egyptians were experts at it, using embalming to preserve royal bodies. Sometimes the circumstances of nature can also preserve a corpse. The perfectly preserved bodies of people who died thousands of years ago have been found in ice and peat bogs. Often the DNA of these long dead people remains partly intact.

at last!

It's all very well being raised from the dead but somehow it's just not the same

If we could clone one of these ancient people, what could they tell us about human life thousands of years ago? Absolutely nothing! Their genetic recipe might be thousands of years old, but memory and experience isn't preserved in the DNA. They'd grow up to be like any other person living in the late 20th century. If someone decided to clone Adolf Hitler, you wouldn't end up with another Hitler. Hitler was a product of his time as much as his genes. His clone would probably end up liking Oasis and The Spice Girls and spending his Saturday nights at the local disco.

If you think that the preservation of long dead humans is impressive, that's nothing compared to some insects which have been found preserved in amber - a hardened tree resin. These insects look as fresh as the day they died, despite the fact that they are tens of millions of years old. Many of these insects were flying when dinosaurs still walked the earth. If any of them dined on a meal of dinosaur blood the day they died, they might still have copies of perfectly preserved dinosaur genetic recipe in their guts. What if we could get at some of this DNA and recreate an entire living dinosaur! Maybe one day, Jurassic Park will become a reality!

Perhaps this is pure science fiction, but if the experiments with Dolly the sheep have taught us anything, it is that yesterday's science fiction can become today's science fact.

MUTANT ANDROIDS GO BESERK IN SLEEPY TOWN IV

We now know that genetics can predict our future, but who can predict the future of genetics? Who knows what else we'll find in our genetic recipes? Genetics has come a long way in its first hundred years. Where will it be in a hundred years from now? Unfortunately, few of us will be around to find out. But maybe that will change if genetics ever gets to grips with life's oldest certainty of all - death. Scientists are convinced that the secret of ageing lies within our genetic recipes. Maybe one day we'll discover the gene for immortality. But who wants to live for ever?

What the words mean

amino acids The chemical building blocks of a protein.

cells The basic units of life. Some organisms, like bacteria, consist of just a single cell. Others, like humans, are made up of billions of cells which form groups of similar cells to make up the different tissues and organs of the body.

chromosomes Thread-like structures in the cell nucleus containing genes.

clone An identical genetic copy. In genetic engineering, cloning normally means to isolate a specific gene and then make copies of it.

DNA A double-stranded molecule - found in almost all living things - which codes for proteins.

dominant gene A gene which is always expressed when present, regardless of its partner gene.

embryo An organism before it emerges from the body of its mother. In humans, the term embryo is specifically used for the first two months of life, after which it is referred to as a foetus.

enzymes Any type of molecule which starts or speeds up chemical reactions in cells.

eugenics The study of the biological improvement of the human race. Popular in the early part of this century, it promoted selectively breeding from those with 'desirable' characteristics while preventing those with 'undesirable' characteristics from breeding. Now largely discredited as racist and unscientific.

fertilization The fusion of male and female sex cells, which combines DNA from the mother and father.

gene A unit of hereditary information. More specifically, a segment of DNA which codes for a protein.

gene therapy A technique to artificially introduce genes into a person's cells, normally used in the treatment of genetic diseases.

genetic engineering The artificial manipulation of genes, usually involving the transfer of genes from one species to another.

genome All the genetic material of a cell.

genotype The genetic 'recipe' of an organism for a particular characteristic.

meiosis Cell division which leaves the daughter cells with half as many chromosomes as the parent cell: the process by which the sex cells are produced.

mitosis Cell division which leaves the daughter cells with the same number of chromosomes as the parent cell: the process by which growth takes place.

mutations Any change in the DNA of a gene.

nucleus The 'control centre' of a cell, this is an inner compartment containing the DNA.

recessive gene A gene that is expressed only when partnered with an identical copy.

Who's who

The list below does not include all of the scientists who have made significant contributions to the progress of genetics, particularly in the years following the discovery of the structure of DNA. There are too many to mention here, and their names and claims to fame can be found elsewhere (see books for further reading on page 127).

Chase, Martha - American scientist who worked with Alfred Hershey (see below).

Crick, Francis - born 1916. The English biologist who, together with James Watson and Maurice Wilkins, discovered the molecular structure of DNA, for which they all received the Nobel prize in 1962. He also helped to show how each DNA sequence of three letters codes for an amino acid, and how the cell uses the DNA code to build proteins.

Galton, Francis - 1822 -1911. Mathematician, traveller, racist. Galton was founder of the study of human inheritance and the eugenics movement, and also established the scientific study of human fingerprints.

Garrod, Sir Archibald - 1857 - 1936. An English doctor who discovered that genetic faults could cause enzyme defects which resulted in rare diseases.

Hershey, Alfred - born 1908. The American bacteriologist who, along with Martha Chase, discovered that DNA was the genetic material. He received the Nobel Prize in 1969.

Mendel, Gregor - 1822-1884. Austrian monk. Working with pea plants, he discovered the basic laws of inheritance and laid the foundations of genetics.

Morgan, Thomas Hunt - 1866-1945. An American biologist who was initially doubtful of Mendel's laws, but his work on fruit flies confirmed them. He showed, amongst other things, that genes were linked to chromosomes.

Watson, James - born 1918. The American who helped discover the structure of DNA and who was, for a time, director of the Human Genome Project.

More information

If you want to keep up to date with what's happening in genetics, the daily newspapers are the best place to start. In Britain, *The Daily Telegraph*, *The Guardian*, and *The Independent* all carry extensive science coverage. *New Scientist* magazine is also a great place to read about the latest news and discoveries.

Any school textbook on biology - or science encyclopedia - will give you basic factual information about DNA and genetics. But if you are interested in the wider implications of the subject, you could try the following:

The Thread of Life - the story of genes and genetic engineering
(1996, Cambridge University Press) by Susan Aldridge
A lively, easy to read, in-depth introduction to genetics.

The Language of the Genes (1993, HarperCollins) by Steve Jones
A fascinating and compelling account of genetics and human evolution.

The Code of Codes (1992, Harvard University Press) by Daniel Kevles and Leroy Hood
An investigation into the scientific and social issues surrounding the Human Genome Project.

The Doctrine of DNA (1992, Penguin) by Richard Lewontin
A superbly written book highlighting the moral and ethical questions facing modern genetics.

WEB SITES

There are hundreds of genetics web sites to explore on the internet. Here are just a few to start you off. All of them contain comprehensive links to other sites.

On-line Mendelian Inheritance in Man (OMIM)
http://www3.ncbi.nlm.nih.gov/omim/
If you want information on any genetic characteristic or genetic disease, this is the place to start.

The Human Genome Project
http://www.ornl.gov/TechResources/HumanGenome/home.html
All you ever wanted to know about the Human Genome Project, plus lots more besides.

Virtual FlyLab
http://vflylab.calstatela.edu/edesktop/VirtApps/VflyLab/
Carry out your own mating experiments on fruit flies!

Blazing a Genetic Trail
http://www.hhmi.org/gentictrail/front/fwd.htm
A fantastic site containing masses of information on the science, history and ethics of genetics.

INDEX